The World Financial System: How It Really Works

I0489970

Lonnie Hicks

ISBN:

13: 978-1500115012 ISBN-10: 1500115010

Real Time Contents

the poor. Audio interview.
Updated: 11/27/13 NSA snooping sex sites and How Wall Street funnels the poor to jail after stealing their homes
Updated: 11/6/13 Bank Deregulation and Economic Crashes. Elizabeth Warren Speaks.
Updated: 7/6/13 An update as of today
Updated: 11/25/12 The World Shadow Banking System: The Video
Updated: 12/13/11 So smarty pants (I hear you say) do you have any ideas about how all this can be fixed? Well yes.
Updated: 12/18/11 The British fire salvos aimed at the big banks. What will the US do?
Updated: 12/20/11 The Federal Reserve Bank proposed reforms. (Make me laugh)
Updated: 12/23/11 Congress engages in insider trading and enrich themselves doing so.

The issue at hand is how the world financial system works.

What are the drivers?

First there are four actors: Governments, the middle class, the poor and the banks.

The middle class and the poor are the major producer of goods of value in systems; they are the only ones who produce anything of value in terms of actual goods. Governments produce valuable services and the banks and Wall Street-like institutions produce very little but trade and make money on the goods produced by the middle class and the poor.

The main driver in the system is population.

The explosion of population around the world was made

possible by the use of oil and oil products. From a population of around two billion, a number which had been stable for centuries, with oil and petroleum we now have a planetary population of roughly 7 billion in a little over 100 years. This is tremendous grow and is now exponential growth. The population is now expected to see accelerated growth to where it may double every 50 years. We will see population explode to 9 billion souls in less than 30 years!

This overall population growth has occurred in less than 200 years, producing an enormous dilemma for governments.

It has produced life style changes of a dubious and unsustainable nature. It has produced famine, war, strides in education true , but all in all it has been a mixed bag and will likely not last.

But it is also clear now also such "strides" endanger the planet and threaten the very existence of the human race.

So how did this occur and what does it have to do with the world financial system?

This explosion of population also created a concomitant need for food, for services, it also resulted in massified institutions.

The massification of society from its rural roots to people crammed in cities has created huge demands on governments for revenue, for food, for planes and tanks to fight wars over resources to keep their populations happy least they be toppled by revolution and uprisings.

Governments needed more than taxation money from the

middle classes and turned to the banks as a way of getting their hands on the needed revenue.

There is this partnership between banks and government which has existed for centuries.

Banks offered ways for the government to get at middle class money beyond taxation. That is, we put our money in the bank every day and that money is loaned in turn back to us, but, most of it goes to loans to governments.

This is the pattern all over the western world.

In order to get the funds governments have had to promise banks that any money lost to commercial loans or even government loans would guaranteed by those very same governments and be paid for by *more taxation* or by growth of their economies.

So banks have been guaranteed an income and no, or low risk, in exchange for their continuing to pass along to government more and more of our money which we have placed into those banks.

All this was supposed to work given steady growth of an economy, and hence, more wealth and jobs and taxes and this would make everything ok.

More growth means more taxes for governments and more wealth being placed into the banks and the governments would get the money back to finance more growth and to pay for more services of a ballooning world population.

All this works, somewhat, until the banks get greedy and keep more than a fair share of the wealth, or until population grows so much that taxation cannot keep up with the needs of that very same population. There busts follow booms, follow busts.

We are now at a situation where no amount of conceivable growth can meet the needs and population driven needs and costs cannot be made up by additional taxations on the middle class and the poor (who pay more in taxes proportionally than the rich.)

We at a point where the third alternative of exploiting third world populations for their resources and cheap labor also cannot make up the difference either.

We at a point where peak oil has occurred and that resource is running out and becoming more and more expensive to dig out of the ground, to the point where we are willing to dig up under the Arctic shelf to find more of the stuff to keep this balloon going.

In Europe the debt crisis, where the banks are bankrupt and have, in turn, bankrupted the governments who guaranteed all of the loans these banks made and these governments have had to, in turn, try to get money from the populations by more taxation, or by reducing the costs of government drastically, which is fact another form of taxation on the middle classes. The poor have been abandoned, and/or incarcerated.

These are the so-called austerity programs now being foisted upon the poor and middle classes in the entire western world.

This is happening as well all over the world, east and west, in the United States as well.

Greed has exacerbated the situation where the super-rich are trying to save themselves and their wealth effectively and now have taken to hoarding middle class deposits, threatening not to loan money to governments, or now use it to exploit and dominate domestic governments or use it to exploit the poor, and/or third world countries to increase their wealth.

Governments tolerate this because they are hoping the rich will loan part of the profits from all this to these same governments to help them keep the wolf from the door. Now mind you, the banks after taking our money, our houses and our treasure, piously tell us we have to cut back and promise to loan our own money back to us at usurious interest rates. Astounding.

None of this mind you, in fact, really works and is a gigantic robbing Peter to pay Paul scheme which periodically collapses.

Now there is a second banking system at work here as well, that is the central banks.

Every country has a version of this hidden shadow banking system.

In the US this is the Federal Reserve Bank. It is neither federal, nor governmental and is fact is the cartel of the largest banks in the United States-Wells, Chase, Citibank, etc.

In 1917, by machination and subterfuge, the US government was duped into creating the system where control of the currency, printing money, is given over to these private banks, who of course, use that power to enrich themselves.

Their power is the power to print money, literally print money, which they then loan to themselves at low or at no interest rates.

This is the manufacturing of money at no cost except the cost of the paper it is printed upon. The dollar bill is not a US treasury note, but is a Federal Reserve note. This should tell you something.

Governments around the world have adopted this shadow banking system because the central banks agreed to lend that paper money to fund the debt of the governments involved. The governments then used the printed money to keep up with the demands of their ever growing populations and to promote growth by giving money back to the super-rich in the form of no, or reduced tax rates and guaranteed profits.

This is the unstated deal between governments and banks.

This is a round robin using middle class money: a Ponzi scheme.

But, this too, is a hidden tax on the middle class in that, if growth does not occur, then inflation is a result; inflation is a tax upon the middle class in a no-growth scenario where wages are flat. US wages have been flat or declining for 30 years while prices have gone up.

If this all seems confusing it is because it is not only confusing but makes no financial sense what so ever.

Note also, that governments loan money to governments as well.

The Chinese have loaned the US government trillions. This

system is, in fact, a world order where the middle class populations of every country support the governments and the banks.

Financial control is now more important than political control; in fact, political control is now subordinated to he who has financial control over middle class/poor populations who really produce the only real wealth on the planet.

All of this is, therefore, as I have described elsewhere, in the end, a gigantic scheme for a few to enrich themselves at the expense of others, using other people's money, that is the money of the poor and middle classes who everyday give the banks their money, their deposits every day, their retirement funds, their savings.

Without those latter actions the system fails because the only real money lies with the 99 percent...

But what to do?

Population is the major driver in all this, and population, it seems, will continue to grow exponentially while resources only grow arithmetically created by the false scarcity and profit mongering capitalism.

This fact is ominous.

We examine possible solutions tomorrow. And there are solutions.

In preparation I have written a bit on this on this site in "What America Needs to Do to Survive" and in my blog on "Obama- The Report Card."

But there is more tomorrow beyond these items written over a year ago.

12/13/11

First in the area of solutions is to examine why this system fails so regularly. There, are of course, many reasons. Here are a few preliminary ones.

1-Putting banks in control of other people's money and no regulation is an obviously bad idea and has failed.

We have to end this. See my blog on this site entitled "The Big Banks: What Are The Alternatives."

2-Much of the issue is unregulated greed and this in turn is fueled by our banking system is based on the fact that everyone in the system is seeking to make a profit on every transaction. This led to banks selling the same mortgage 50 times (derivatives) over to various customers, something that makes no sense financially or otherwise and is outright fraud; which the banks fully knew as they placed big bets that these derivatives would fail and they did. In fact the banks had a financial interest in that failure through "re-insurance schemes (AIG.) This is what is known as "hedging."

And these phony derivatives did fail and the banks made billions on them this over and above what they got in bail outs.

That is why they recovered so quickly. They are betting on failure again, betting that America will go bust, and will get rich if America does, and are in a position to make sure their bets come true by their daily manipulations of the markets. Governments tolerate this because they get some of that money demanding that banks buy, say, US treasury notes.

But the damage done in 2008 did not go away--over 700 trillion in these now worthless derivatives are still out unpaid and is debt hidden on the balance sheets of banks around the world. (Some estimate the number, if we include private equity funds, at a quadrillion dollars.)

3-The last of these preliminary solutions include creating, a non-profit banking system with real controls on the for-profit banks.

4-Stop giving the predatory banks our money every day and put our money in local banks with the proviso that this money be invested locally to create jobs locally.

The state bank of North Dakota is an example of a state-owned, not profit bank that has been in place for decades and really serves the citizens of that state as opposed to exploiting them.

That state has no recession.

More over California and cities are now looking into municipal and state banks where the contagion of profit with other people's money is taken out of the equation. See my article "The Big Banks-What Are the Alternatives?" on this site.

5. Launch a federal program to fund local banks through the Community Reinvestment Act which currently exists. This act requires that banks set aside 1% of their deposits for local investments and local economic development. Since small businesses produce most of the jobs in this

country, not corporations, it makes sense to put 150 billion into this program.

Currently the conservatives are trying to kill this program but it, in fact, should be expanded. A catch, however, is that the presidents of the big banks and the federal reserve actually run this program and might resist more money being put into this effort. It should be done regardless, and is a fight worth fighting for.

More soon.

12/18/11

Solutions UK style. These will be imitated in the United States. They are logical ones to pursue.

I will discuss these solutions in a later blog.

http://www.bbc.co.uk/news/business-16235636

http://www.bbc.co.uk/news/business-12391532

12-20-11

 The US banks, via the Federal Reserve are now following the proposed UK banking reforms. Too little too late?

http://www.bbc.co.uk/news/business-16280175

 http://www.bbc.co.uk/news/business-16239255

2/22/11

For a peek at the round robin process I have described above see the NY Times article below. The authors describe this in the context of governments, and banks trying to deal with the Euro Debt Crisis and in doing so we get a rare peak behind the green curtain at OZ.

http://www.nytimes.com/2011/12/22/business/global/demand-for-ecb-loans-surpasses-

expectations.html?pagewanted=1&_r=2&hp

Will this proposed solution work in Europe and in the United States? I will evaluate this tomorrow and the other proposed reforms as well.

A hint: You cannot solve debt problems by adding on more debt.

12/23/11

Insider trading is legal for congress people. See link:

http://www.booktv.org/Program/13109/Throw+Them+All+Out+How+Politicians+and+Their+Friends+Get+Rich+Off+Insider+Stock+Tips+Land+Deals+and+Cronyism+That+Would+Send+the+Rest+of+Us+to+Prison.aspx

Salt to the wound if these insider trades go bad, often we the taxpayers have to pay for it all.

http://thehill.com/business-a-lobbying/199523-insider-trading-bill-advances-in-senate-over-gop-opposition

The above bill, odds are, will be in the end, watered down or killed.

9/15/12

Here is a case study showing exactly how the world financial systems works--it's showed up in the 2008 financial crisis.

http://news.goldseek.com/GoldSeek/1347653228.php

11/25/12

The World Shadow Banking System-How it Works.

http://www.youtube.com/watch?feature=player_detailpage&v=XliTvxqTtsE

http://rt.com/shows/keiser-report/episode-466-max-keiser-651/

11/6/13

Bank Deregulation and Economic Crashes. Elizabeth Warren Speaks.

 http://www.youtube.com/watch?feature=player_detailpage&v=nTWfa-iO9Nc

11/27/13
How Wall Street has created the incarceration nation. And more on NSA

http://www.alternet.org/corporate-accountability-and-workplace/how-wall-st-turned-america-incarceration-nation

http://www.alternet.org/news-amp-politics/top-secret-documents-reveal-nsa-spied-porn-habits-radicals-discredit-them?akid=11195.260128.HbUMUF&rd=1&src=newsletter930023&t=5

4/14/14
How the rich and the banks have shifted the tax burden from themselves to the middle class and the poor.

http://www.kpfa.org/archive/id/101825

http://www.kpfa.org/archive/id/101906

http://www.authorsden.com/visit/viewshortstory.asp?id=59959&authorid=121255

http://www.authorsden.com/visit/viewshortstory.asp?id=59959&authorid=121255

http://www.authorsden.com/visit/viewshortstory.asp?id=54195&authorid=121255

http://www.authorsden.com/visit/viewshortstory.asp?id=49909&authorid=121255

4/14/14

"Who pays federal taxes?

Last year, the federal government collected $2.8 trillion in taxes and fees. Here is where the money came from:

— Individual income tax: 47 percent.

— Payroll taxes: 32 percent.

— Corporate income tax: 10 percent.

— Excise taxes: 3 percent.

— Unemployment insurance: 2 percent

— Estate and gift taxes: 1 percent.

— Customs duties: 1 percent.

— Miscellaneous: 4 percent.

Sources: IRS, AP-GfK Poll conducted March 20-24, Treasury report on budget year 2013."

From:

http://bostonherald.com/news_opinion/national/2014/04/april_15_not_much_of_a_deadline_for_most_taxpayers

40 years ago it was reversed. Corporations paid at a 91 percent tax rate 47 percent of the taxes.

Since they only pay 10% of the taxes now, guess who has had to make up the rest: individuals have been burdened with the payroll taxes, the unemployment taxes, the Medicare taxes and now we are paying 82 percent of the taxes. What is wrong with this picture?

4/18/14

Too Big to Fail and Too Big To Go To Jail

http://www.alternet.org/books/matt-taibbi-superrichamerica-have-become-untouchables-america-who-dont-go-prison

4/18/14

The American Dream is now dead?

https://www.youtube.com/watch?feature=player_detailpage&v=pyVmoCxnGyk

4/26/14

The Piketty Study on Inequality. New and influential Study

http://www.nationofchange.org/now-we-know-economic-inequality-malady-and-not-cure-1398519838

5.2/14

The Secret World lf Hedge Funds and how they have sold out America

"Prominent hedge funds are helping to fuel the wave of so-called inversion deals that are structured to lower tax rates by moving the domiciles of U.S. companies, particularly those operating in the pharmaceuticals sector, to foreign jurisdictions like Ireland. It's pretty clear that Wall Street has cheered on the inversion trend, feasting on the investment banking fees generated by these deals, and that the markets even enjoy an increase in price of the stocks of both the seller and the buyer on the day the deals get announced".

Now if these huge companies dodge taxes in the US the US taxpayer has to make up the difference in taxes we pay here at home, and more, a weakened tax base means more austerity programs for the US population and a weaken political system becomes even more dependent upon corporate money.

This is a win-win for companies who already have parked over 1.2 trillion dollars overseas already! They have refused to bring or invest that money back home, furthering economic chaos in the US. This is tantamount to economic treason, all the while using their dollars to encourage "patriotism" among these same beleaguered Americans they are fleecing.

5/9/14

How Wall Street is and did bankrupt America's Cities

http://www.nationofchange.org/la-story-s-all-too-familiar-1399646753

5/11/14 What is wrong with Welfare?

"That means in 2014, a family of four earning $11,925 a year likely got less aid than a same-sized family earning $47,700."

From:

http://www.sciencedaily.com/releases/2014/05/140506130259.htm

Is wall street rigged? NY AG thinks so.

By **Ed Silverstein**

High-frequency trading is getting   scrutinized by the New York Attorney General's office - as investigations involving federal authorities continue into the controversial practice.

Among the firms named in a *Wall Street Journal* report are Goldman Sachs, Barclays and Credit Suisse, as AG Eric Schneiderman's office decides if high-frequency trading firms had advantages over other investors through private venues run by the banks, known as "dark pools."

His office wants the banks to provide information that could show if high-speed firms had "secret arrangements," the report said. Such arrangements may give firms unfair preferences in making trades.

In total, some half-dozen banks could be investigated by the state's Attorney General's office, news reports said.

And Goldman Sachs' private stock-trading venue "Sigma X" could be closed down, according to news reports - but no decision on its future has been made.

Meanwhile, the Securities and Exchange Commission, the Department of Justice and the Federal Bureau of investigation are looking at high-speed trading, as well. In particular, the DOJ and FBI may be looking at whether the almost instant trades violate insider trading regulations, according to Fortune.

Note that the pension fund people, state funds, union pension funds, all pension fund managers, banks, all keep quiet about all this because the managers of these funds benefit from wall street and the retires only find out about it 40 years later when they try to retire and find out they have accumulated only 1 percent interest over these years, house underwater, heavily in debt, school and credit card debt. How did this happen? What is the history even beyond 40 years ago? See the stunning video below.

5/12/14

How the Rich Took Over America and Tricked US into the Federal Reserve System and Endless Wars

Stunning Video

https://www.youtube.com/watch?feature=player_detailpage&v=p6I6L8b6mQs

5/13/14

The Crisis of the American Empire in the 21st Century, and the Rich

http://www.counterpunch.org/2014/05/13/the-federal-reserve-and-an-unsustainable-empire/)

5/15/14

The Federal Reserve Bank in American and English History Video

https://www.youtube.com/watch?feature=player_detailpage&v=RzoP4iMICO4

The Deficit: The Facts

http://www.authorsden.com/visit/viewshortstory.asp?id=50518

Meritocracy of the Poor and Middle Class?

http://www.nationofchange.org/evidence-meritocracy-made-poor-people-1400511508

Do we really need Wall Street Banks? What are the laws preventing reform?

http://truth-out.org/news/item/23781-are-private-banks-unconstitutional

5/23/14

How are average citizens doing in the US and in the Uk? Their financial future?

http://www.youtube.com/watch?feature=player_detailpage&v=NWtRgW4cjjY

5/27/14

What's happening and going to happen in World Finances? Take a look.

Quadrillion in Derivative Debt-

"A derivative, put simply, is a contract between two parties whose value is determined by changes in the value of an underlying asset. Those assets could be bonds, equities, commodities or currencies. The majority of contracts are traded over the counter, where details about pricing, risk measurement and collateral, if any, are not available to the public.

In other words, a derivative does not have any intrinsic value."

"According to official government numbers, the top 25 banks in the United States now have a grand total of more than 236 trillion dollars of exposure to derivatives. But there are four banks that dwarf everyone else. The following are the latest numbers for those four banks...

JPMorgan Chase

Total Assets: $1,945,467,000,000 (nearly 2 trillion dollars)

Total Exposure To Derivatives: $70,088,625,000,000 **(more than 70 trillion dollars)**

Citibank

Total Assets: $1,346,747,000,000 (a bit more than 1.3 trillion dollars)

Total Exposure To Derivatives: $62,247,698,000,000 **(more than 62 trillion dollars)**

Bank Of America

Total Assets: $1,433,716,000,000 (a bit more than 1.4 trillion dollars)

Total Exposure To Derivatives: $38,850,900,000,000 **(more than 38 trillion dollars)**

Goldman Sachs

Total Assets: $105,616,000,000 (just a shade over 105 billion dollars – yes, you read that correctly)

Total Exposure To Derivatives: $48,611,684,000,000 (**more than 48 trillion dollars**)"

From:

http://theeconomiccollapseblog.com/archives/the-size-of-the-derivatives-bubble-hanging-over-the-global-economy-hits-a-record-high

See also:

http://www.bis.org/publ/otc_hy1405.htm

5/30/14

Why Currency Wars Matter to You
https://www.youtube.com/watch?feature=player_detailpage&v=cs1Xwm1TuIM

Update: 5/3114

The Financial History of the World 4 hour video

https://www.youtube.com/watch?feature=player_detailpage&v=4Xx_5PuLIzc

5/31/14

The US Financial System as a Scam

https://www.youtube.com/watch?feature=player_detailpage&v=iFDe5kUUyT0

6/2/14

http://www.theguardian.com/money/2014/jun/02/los-angeles-racist-mortgage-lending-big-banks

Happy New Year? I'll Get Back to You On That. (Do not read this while happy.)

Updated: 7/23/13 Wall Street moves to head off financial transaction tax
Updated: 7/21/13 How commodity trading by wall street affects your everyday life and started Arab Spring.
Updated: 7/20/13 Elizabeth Warren ruffling feathers in the Senate
Updated: 7/18/13 Supreme Court Millionaires. Who influences Them?
Updated: 7/11/13 EU and the US reach a deal on trading derivatives. What?
Updated: 7/11/13 Why did the Fed give European Banks 13 trillion dollars since 2008?
Updated: 7/10/13 The False Numbers on Jobs in America and Plutocracy-The Video
Updated: 7/10/13 Inside JP Morgan: who are the players and what is the history?
Updated: 7/8/13 New Capital Requirements Proposed for big banks?
Updated: 7/8/13 EU approves stealing money directly for bank accounts of consumers.

Updated: 7/6/13 The Demographic Time Bomb facing all of Europe, Japan China, and the US

Updated: 7/5/13 Black teen unemployment rate 95% Unbelievable.

Updated: 7/3/13 World's Largest Banks to be charged with collusion-who's who list of the so-soon to investigated

Updated: 7/1/13 America's Middle Class lowest in the world except for Russia?

Updated: 6/30/13 Big banks will not be able to stand up in financial crisis without bringing down the entire system--says regulators.

Updated: 6/29/13 Mortgages Jump by the most in 26 years?

Updated: 6/29/13 Gold falls to new three year low in price. Why?

Updated: 6/28/13 A prediction on what will happen this year.

Updated: 6/28/13 The Re-Colonization of Africa?

Updated: 6/26/13 This blog was started to predict what will happen in the next two years. It has happened.

Updated: 6/25/13 Senators propose to end Fannie Mae and Freddie Mac. What does it mean for your mortgage?

Updated: 6/24/13 76% of Americans living pay check to pay check?

Updated: 6/22/13 Bank stocks sink like a stone.

Updated: 6/22/13 What do banks do with the 85 billion a month given to them by the Federal Reserve?

Updated: 6/21/13 Supreme Court backs Corporations over US Consumers

Updated: 6/20/13 New Report in England on Banks. Recommends jail.

Updated: 6/19/13 The Eminent Domain Movement Comes to California

Updated: 6/19/13 America's disappearing middle class- 27th in the world

Updated: 6/19/13 Bank of America former employees file suit claiming bank told them to lie about foreclosures.

Updated: 6/18/13 Africa the next boom continent?

Updated: 6/17/13 Why hasn't a single wall street executive been prosecuted and/, or gone to jail?

Updated: 6/14/13 Obama caves in to Wall Street again. Derivatives still running rampant?

6/12/13 Where have the jobs gone. A flawed MIT study on the subject

6/10/13 How tech companies and wall street have stolen the future of our youth world-wide

6/7/13 What will happen in 2014- A Detailed Scenario- "The painful price of subsidized money

6/4/13 Money as Fetish

6/1/13 Why do we continue to allow the banks to run the federal reserve for their own profit?

6/1/13 Confiscation of depositor accounts now the new normal and time for public banks?

5/26/13 Wall Street Tries to Kill Financial Reform

5/24/13 Who Voted to Keep JP Morgan Chief in his dual roles and why.

5/24/13 Wall Street Lobbyists are writing the financial reform implementation rules. Yep.

5/23/13 The IRS Scandal-What is it about

5/21/13 Jamie Dimon beats back stockholder revolt.

5/10/13 Who is getting screwed in the social security scene?

5/6/13 NY Attorney General suing two big banks over failure to follow through on mortgage settlement.

5/5/13 Are offshore profits enough to fund the sequester?

5/4/13 Obama offering cuts to Medicare? Say it isn't so.

4/18/13 How five years of bailout have robbed seniors of their life savings.

1/2/13 It is Prediction Season--Here are some initial ones from me. Pension, Bonds, and Financial Chaos

1/1/13 After the Fiscal Cliff What Now?

12/31/12 What are the details of a Fiscal Cliff Deal?

12/28/12 American Civil Liberties take it on the chin.

12/27/12 Who gets what percentage of profits in American corporations? What has been the history and the changes over time?

12/30/12 Inside the Fiscal Cliff Negotiations, today Sunday 12/30/12

12/28/12 Obama Care Provisions due to come in effect in 2013? What are they?

12/21/12 What Budget cuts are being proposed in the Obama 2013 budget and to which programs?

12/20/12 Only one of the two "Plan B" bills passes. What does it all mean?

12/20/12 What is really in Plan B-the Republican plan-and what is left out?

12/19/12 Obama is offering Wall Street a cut of social security benefits? I think so.

12/18/12 The latest offers in the fiscal cliff thing. Obama giving ground?

12/9/12 The Fiscal Cliff-Best Video on the Issues

11/28/12 The World Shadow Banking System-The Video

11/19/12 What is the end game of the monied classes.

Greece? And, the Debt Resistors Manual

10/1/12 New Bank regulator in England vows that bankers will repent or go to jail. If so London will set a trend?

9/29/12 How is QE3 going so far? Does it make any sense?

Updated: 9/29/12 What was the Great Depression of 1929 like?

Updated: 9/29/12 European Financial Transactions Tax gains momentum.

Updated: 9/28/12 Bush tax cuts caused the deficit? Apparently.

Updated: 9/28/12 Who works less, is taxed more, has less recession and spend less time in school--Guess who?

9/28/12 The French set to tax the rich at 75% rate-will this work in the US. Yes this author says

9/11/12 My predictions on Global Finance

9/4/12 Five triggers which could ignite financial trouble

9/3/12 What will the triggers be for US and Global Finance upheavals for the rest of this year and next? What to do?

9/2/12 Where did the deficit come from, who got rich off of it now and then?

9/1/12 Well What are the events which will dominate 2013-Let's start with Private Equity

6/16/12 What is The New World Order? Some people claim they know. Eight videos

Updated: 6/5/12 How Congress and Europe directly affect your pocketbook and what will happen this year to your wallet.

Updated: 6/4/12 George Soros Rings the Financial Alarm Bells

Updated: 1/2/12 Depression in America? We have only three years to avert it.

Updated: 1/15/12 Greece will likely default. Oh, oh.

Wall Street Retaliates Against Sarkozy and his government will fall as a result.

January is forecast month and the forecast for the European Common Market is grim to grimmer.

See links below to get an idea and then I'll look at it from the standpoint of its impact upon the United States and the price of gold and silver.

http://www.bbc.co.uk/news/business-16301630

http://www.bbc.co.uk/news/world-europe-16377010

Understand one thing: Crisis and bad economic times always benefit elites and "investors" who have cash.

For example note that the interest rates being demanded by American investors using our money is 6-7 percent for the PIIGS (Portugal, Ireland, Greece, Italy, Spain, is high and assets in these countries are cheap. All this while paying Americans only 1-2 percent on their own money. Wow, how peculiar.

Meantime, you generally might see gold and silver prices go up and down as these "investors" put cash in and out of gold and silver, temporarily, in order to purchase the cheap assets of these now near bankrupt countries. They win on high interest rates and get to purchase cheap assets using our money while paying us nothing interest on our own money, to boot get to keep any profits from all this and if these investments fail they can send the bill to us the taxpayers, the very ones who gave them the money in the first place.

This, Virginia, is the way of the world; it is also what causes rebellions if not revolutions.

Tomorrow, a look at the impact this is likely to have on this country where we will also go to detail about all of this.

1/2/12

This run away and selling off from gold and silver was instigated in part by the announcement by the Federal Reserve of the United States and the European Central bank that they would fund the banks of Europe 640 billion Euros in the case of the latter and perhaps a trillion dollars in the case of the former.

So European banks get trillions of dollars and Euros in aid and three year low or no cost loans from the taxpayers of the United States and Europe; these Central banks do this by printing money, (remember these central banks control the printing of money in the US and in Europe) this money printing will surely create rising inflation which will result in rising prices for the middle classes of these countries which in effect is a hidden tax on the middle classes--of course making the recession worse, not better.

What is going on is that the monied classes know this perfectly well and are trying to buy up the assets of the bankrupt countries (I include the US in this as well) before these rising prices actually occur three years down the road.

And they are doing it with our money which they had placed in gold and silver. Here is why. Deficits and bankruptcy means they charge usurious interest rates to these countries seeking loans. Take a look at their current demands in terms of interest rates.

Diverging fortunes

Rate at which markets are willing to lend to governments for 10 years:

- **Germany**: 2.05%

- **France**: 2.83%

- **Spain**: 4.95%

- **Italy**: 5.56%

- **Irish Republic**: 7.41%

- **Portugal**: 10.80%

- **Greece**: 22.14%

So they are taking every dime they have to buy up low-cost PIIGS assets before prices rise and to simultaneously charge outrageous rates. If the countries don't pay they simply foreclose and buy up that countries assets, usually with government's willingly cooperating, since these governments are under the thumb of the banks and lenders anyway.

This is normal operating procedure for these economic terrorists.

Millions will suffer in the US and Europe, as they realize that their country has been literally sold off to the wall streets of the world, their water rights, their schools, their productive industries all will be sold to private investors by their governments, governments obviously controlled by the debt mongers and the predatory banks.

Recession, (let's call it what it is--on-coming depression) will be a holocaust for an already devastated middle class on both continents.

Meantime the British, the real culprits in the phony derivative debacle, have essentially refused to have these speculations curtailed because in England *there is no law limiting how many times a derivative can be sold and re-*

sold using the same collateral (i.e. a mortgage.)

The current average in London is *400 times* the collateral involved. In the US the average is 140 times. This is astounding.

That is why the British have resisted a speculation transactions tax, one that Sarkozy and Merkel support in order to prevent predatory banks from making Germany and France into another Greece.
The English economy is literally dependent upon continuing these fraudulent financial practices to the extent that England is willing to drop valuable contacts and trade with the ECM.

But, you say, what can be done.?
Ah, something can be done, but it has to be done in the next three years.

But what about the US and the impact of all this on the US?

That tomorrow, but note that Europe is the major trading partner of the United States, and that is why the Federal Reserve is putting trillions into the banks in Europe to save them. It is in the interest of our banks here to do so, not the middle class, but the banks.

Our banks don't want the European banks to default on money that our banks have loaned those European banks. And they want to make sure that some cash is still there after these European banks have paid out money to the PIIGS.

You see how all of the convoluted system works? It doesn't make any sense in the end and these bankers know it. They are only looking to save their own bacon in the short run, store up their wealth, and to hell with the rest of the world.

Sad but true.

See:

http://www.bbc.co.uk/news/business-14934728

But there are remedies. Just as they have given themselves an extra three years, we too have three years to do something about it all.

More later.

1/13/12

 The Euro Lemmings continue their march to the sea. France's credit rating is downgraded. Will look at this later.

http://www.bbc.co.uk/news/business-16556860
http://www.bbc.co.uk/news/business-16553532

Now note that if Greece defaults on its debt, and/or drops out of the Eurozone, trouble abounds. But with the granting of trillions in dollars and billions in Euro's by the central bank of the zone and by our Federal Reserve the end can be postponed and perhaps avoided for at least three years.

Greece in the end could be a big winner, and the American taxpayer the big loser.

France's credit rating is down will sink further, dragging Germany along to the bottom, especially in light of the Greece likely default.

It is not the end of the world, but from where I am standing, I can see the edge. We have time to back off that edge only if we re-gain our sanity and devise a plan to save Europe our major trading partner.

More later.

1/16/12
Things are developing fast on the European front.

Yesterday the above articles reported on the lowering of France's credit rating and on the possibility of a Greek formal default.

But we are not told why this has occurred in the French example. First thing to know is that this was no accident.

You'll recall I detailed above that Sarkozy and Merkel led the fight to install a greed and speculation tax on American speculators.

The British refused to go along with this tax idea, protecting their bankers.

But Wall Street got angry at Sarkozy, the lead advocate of this tax and is retaliating against him because he led the fight. Obama and Gietner several months ago went to France to lobby against the idea joining the British in the effort.

Now understand that the rating agencies are controlled by wall street. Wall street banks literally pay the salaries of these rating agencies. The pretend myth is that they are independent of the Street, is just that-a myth.

The game is the following:

1. A lower rating at this point is a blow to Sarkozy 100 days from his re-election, a re-election in which he vowed not to have France have its credit rating lowered. Unpopular already, he is mostly likely to lose the election and be out of the way.

2. Now a second shoe here is the banks now have a rationale to up the borrowing rate on the French meaning financial turmoil is now added to the mix and injury to injury they make money on the higher interest rates they themselves will demand. No justice here. No conflict of interest here.

3. Social turmoil is also more likely since this means more austerity for the French middle class, and strengthens the hand of right wing elements in France.

4. This is not unusual. This is standard operating procedure in the cut-throat financial world. The bankers and their rating agency minions did it to Obama, did it to Greece

and Italy as well. Toppling governments that do not please them is happening more and more frequently and now more and more they are doing it openly.

5. This is also a warning shot across Merkel's bow in as much as she can't tax the Germans more in an election year and more debt is something that the German middle class will not tolerate. Let's see if Merkel fights on or not.

Such is the world.

6/4/12
Apparently George Soros agrees with the above analysis: See below

http://m.bbc.co.uk/news/business-18320881

 Are the bankers being sued for trillions in new lawsuit?

http://www.youtube.com/watch?v=5JDcv01ar-k&src_vid=lxLcDiiFfCM&annotation_id=annotation_966632&feature=iv

6/5/12
Think that the European Debt Crisis has not much to do with you sitting on the couch at home? Think again. Remember "depositors" means you and my paycheck in Chase, Wells BofA and virtually all banks...

http://www.foxbusiness.com/personal-finance/2012/06/07/5-ways-jpmorgan-troubles-may-affect/

http://thehill.com/blogs/pundits-blog/economy-a-budget/230891-europes-contagious-debt-crisis

And more: How what Congress does or does not do in six months will directly affect your pocket book. Link and quotes below.

http://thehill.com/blogs/congress-blog/economy-a-budget/230763-the-fiscal-train-wrecks-awaiting-us-unless-congress-acts

"**Personal tax rates** - Everybody's, let me repeat, everybody's personal taxes will go up in 2013 by thousands of dollars. The lowest 10% individual income tax bracket will expire, reverting to 15%. The highest 35% individual income tax rate will rise higher to 39.6%. People in between will see a 3% hike in their tax rate, on average. The overall heightening of taxes – income, payroll, health care taxes, etc. -- will suck $399 billion from the economy and into the government coffers."

"**Capital gains and dividends rates** - The 0% and 15% tax rates on long-term capital gains will expire, rising to 10% for lower tax brackets and to 20% for higher tax brackets. The current qualified dividend tax rates of 0% for lower tax brackets and 15% for higher tax brackets will rise to ordinary income tax rates for all individuals. Higher capital gains taxes means less investment, which means fewer jobs."

Of course the conclusion of this article is biased. Congressional inaction on jobs will create more job loss is the fact. More government income is needed to produce the dollars needed to put people to work, is my view, and that is also the view of most economists, and this is exactly what was done in the last great depression to bring us out of it.

Poor and middle class people are now living pay check to pay check and upon getting a job will spend the money and thus companies hire more people because there is profit to be made and the economy grows. There is no growth if people are out of work and make no mistake austerity puts people out of work.

Notice above that the tax rate for wealthy individuals is 0% and a low 15% for capital gains including those speculating with our money.

Zero percent!

The average millionaire in this country pays only 15% in taxes and that doesn't count the money on taxes that would be collected if the government forced corporations to repatriate their profits from overseas tax shelters. It doesn't count tax evasion savings accrued in this fashion.

Dividends are not taxed at all in some cases. Who gets dividends? The rich mostly.

So the tax schedules are skewed in favor of the wealthy while the average American pays 21 to 30 percent of their income in taxes with no way to reduce that bill by hiding income overseas.

The rationale used is that these folks will invest their tax breaks and create jobs. Well we see how that has worked out. What they did in fact was to take our money(our money because we have to make up for the taxes they don't pay by higher taxes upon ourselves and having the government borrow money to cover these tax losses) and gamble with it and lost it almost bringing the world finance system to ruin. And, they are set to do this again.

Clearly extreme budgeting and austerity programs don't work as the European example illustrates.

http://www.nytimes.com/2012/06/07/us/politics/democrats-get-line-of-attack-in-europes-woes.html?ref=politics

My remedy is simple. Stop giving these folks our money and let us keep our own money to invest locally in our own communities.

6/11/12

Some people say that the takeover of Greece, Spain, Ireland and the rest is the prototype for a new world order dominated by bankers and elites.

They argue that what we are witnessing is the end of democracy in Europe where major decisions are made by the IMF, The European Central Bank and the like. Individuals don't elect these folks yet they dominate major decisions and the populations suffer. They argue that the same thing is slowing happening in the United States as well.

See what you think. Here are the six videos and then we get back and discuss.
http://www.youtube.com/watch?v=4PpMdTmVMpo&feature=youtube_gdata_player

http://www.youtube.com/watch?v=mLdpvSRNZLk&feature=youtube_gdata_player

http://www.youtube.com/watch?v=LnSFTZfUI_I&feature=youtube_gdata_player

http://www.youtube.com/watch?v=FmeH32STov0&feature=youtube_gdata_player

http://www.youtube.com/watch?v=1-0xBqHZf_M&feature=youtube_gdata_player

http://www.youtube.com/watch?v=T40GNlckRl8&feature=youtube_gdata_player

http://www.youtube.com/watch?v=e5kDMsrorwI&feature=youtube_gdata_player

http://www.youtube.com/watch?v=pWVFodWh5B0&feature=youtube_gdata_player

http://www.youtube.com/watch?v=yT1GavDtiwM&feature=player_detailpage

9/1/12

Private Equity Firms Under Scrutiny by NY Attorney

General for Tax strategies-Bain capital involved as well as some of the largest equity firms in the country. Subpoenas already have been issued.

"The tax strategy — which is viewed as perfectly legal by some tax experts, aggressive by others and potentially illegal by some — came to light last month when hundreds of pages of Bain's internal financial documents were made available online. The financial statements show that at least $1 billion in accumulated fees that otherwise would have been taxed as ordinary income for Bain executives had been converted into investments producing capital gains, which are subject to a federal tax of 15 percent, versus a top rate of 35 percent for ordinary income. That means the Bain partners saved more than $200 million in federal income taxes and more than $20 million in Medicare taxes.

http://www.nytimes.com/2012/09/02/business/inquiry-on-tax-strategy-adds-to-scrutiny-of-finance-firms.html?_r=1&partner=rss&emc=rss

Who is on the subpoena list?

"Among the firms to receive subpoenas are Kohlberg Kravis Roberts & Company, TPG Capital, Sun Capital Partners, Apollo Global Management, Silver Lake Partners and Bain Capital,"

"Clayton, Dubilier & Rice; Crestview Partners; H.I.G. Capital; Vestar Capital Partners; and Providence Equity Partners."

9/2/12

World Debt-Who Caused it-Who Got the Money-and Who has to pay it back.

The world we live in is a construction of the banks using phony debt as a means of control.

So let's have a look at the debt leader-the United States.
How did this happen?
How did this debt happen?

First let's today settle the question of who or what caused the deficit in the United States in the first place such that the government had to borrow all that money and who got rich of the debt we currently have.

First a little history of debt in this country and then we go to the specifics.

Turns out the greatest contributor to the greatest debt in in US history was George Bush.

See below: Debt increased from 133 billion to 1 trillion dollars during his administration. This was the Republican "starve the beast" strategy--create a debt ridden government and then under the cover of austerity take back middle class assets, ignoring the fact that two wars made

Republican defense contractors, the banks, , the pentagon, the so-called security industry and wall street--rich. There is no justice here.

On top of all this is the claim that the middle class overspent and now has to tighten its belt because the monied classes simultaneously reduced wages forcing the middle class to put their wives, children and grannies to work and use their high interest rate credit cards to survive.

Why can't the American public see this scam is beyond me.

But a chart is worth a thousand words.

http://jimcgreevy.com/gvdc/Natl_Debt_Chart.html

It is clear that the Republicans ran up the debt with bailouts for banks, two wars, and tax breaks for the rich.

I am suggesting this was and is no accident.

And they are poised to do it again because there are billions in profits in it for their constituents-the banks, the pentagon, the so-called security industry, the prison industrial industry, and the war profiteers.

Tomorrow let's go back for more detail and a prognosis on the above which is clearly not sustainable. It will be a re-run of 1929. See the PBS video special on the 1929 debacle to get a look at how it all worked then.

http://www.pbs.org/wgbh/americanexperience/films/crash/

9/3/12

So what will be the critical events in 2013 and will there
be financial collapse as some are predicting?

What happens to global finance next year and in the
finance situation in the United States--and what will be the
triggers?

Will there be change? You bet.

Let's first talk about the basic problems and then solutions.

(Note: I am not going to be talking about buying gold.
Most people can't afford it and the oft-made point is that '
You can't eat gold or silver" is accurate.)
Countries may buy gold but real people can't and shouldn't.
This idea in the end is just another recommendation
designed to get the people invested in gold and silver
richer. That is not you and I. It is the same wall street
moguls mentioned above. So skip this.

Secondly we will have a look at real world and historical
default and currency debasement-like that predicted for
Greece. What actually happens on the ground and has
happened historically?
Is the end of world?

It is for the monied classes but not for ordinary people, and
we have the example of a successful currency change in
Argentina. Sure the creditors lost their money but so what;

Argentina now currently thrives.

In fact we have had currency changes in the United States as well, from the colonial currencies, to the confederate currency etc. Did the world fall apart? No, it did not.

The idea that it will comes from these same monied classes trying to protect their fortunes.

Thirdly, we look at the issue/warning that rampant inflation will occur and how horrible that will be. Besides higher, reasonable interest rates keep the bank speculators from getting free money at zero percent. We don't get any interest anyway from these characters (1% over the last 10 years) so we might as well keep our money locally in our own communities and put it to work there creating jobs. Stop giving them our money is clearly the right thing to do.

But what is the real world experience?

Most times the example of the Weinmar Republic (Germany) is brought up as the horror story of what can happen, stories of currency inflation such that prices were raised three times a day and people had to take wheelbarrows of money to the store to buy groceries.

Well, who gets hurt in rampant inflation?

Mostly the rich-the creditors.

The middle classes can and will change to a new currency and suddenly the 200k mortgage can be paid back in two years rather than in thirty 30 years with the inflated currency.

That is why you hear the conservative-dominated press and economists rail so much against inflation--because the monied classes lose big. Note too the connection between inflation and growth in that devaluated dollars means more exports hence more jobs and note currency is just paper. Look at how it was done in Argentina and in Germany, an economy now stronger than ever despite horror stories about the Weinmar republic.

And that is the lesson here for the monied classes-share the wealth or it will be shared in other, uglier ways-but it will be shared.

Right now the monied classes clearly would rather see Marshal Law, internal occupation of the American population rather than share their ill-gotten gains.

Now the bottom line fact is that there is literally not enough money in the world to repay these phony debts, consumer or national, and the debts will have to be forgiven largely or by another way go into default. Elites will fight this of course. That is their history.

Look at history: few elites have been enlightened enough to share; that is the origin of this very American republic and why we had to have a revolution against the Crown which was protecting the interests of the Bank of England

and the merchant classes because in that time these institutions were bankrolling the Crown itself in its pursuit of wars with the French and other countries.

So thanks for the patience, let's get on with the analysis, first thing tomorrow we look at the triggers for the rest of this year and next and what can be done to protect ourselves.

9/4/12

Pensioners defrauded of their life savings.

http://www.youtube.com/watch?list=PL768846B770CB8C95&v=8xK1ljgnvQE&feature=player_detailpage

http://www.youtube.com/watch?list=PL768846B770CB8C95&v=UgnqBOarHHw&feature=player_detailpage

9/4/12

What will be the triggers for the rest of the year and the consequences in global and US finance?

Well there are several. Let's list a few first and the go back after for the detail.

1. 70% of the trades on Wall Street are by computer. Computer glitches real or manipulated can set off a panic and that can make valuations and pricing difficult if not impossible, including gold, silver and stocks.

2. The Greek default could result in currency debasement. This would have a domino effect in the west. If not Greece then if Spain asks for a postponement of its austerity programs. Both could trigger in a month or two. Trouble.

3. The rising price of fuel, food and jobs is what actually set off the "Arab Spring" riots. Egypt is at that point again. The most dangerous point for a country as far as bloody revolution is concerned is when seeming gains that are followed by severe setbacks-Egypt is in this group.

It was fuel prices and food price increases which set off the Arab spring and it will be rising food and fuel prices that will do it again.

See my blog on the rapid increase in worldwide food and fuel prices and who caused it all.

http://www.authorsden.com/visit/viewshortstory.asp?AuthorID=121255&id=50904

How close are they to more increases?

Close.

Governments around the world subsidize fuel and food prices already to avoid revolution-prices controlled by the banks. These two (fuel and food) plus arms purchases are what these countries spend their money on.

4. April is the deadline when the US government receipts

in taxation come in. If lower than anticipated then expect the US credit rating to drop and interest rates to drop below zero etc., and perhaps a run on US securities and perhaps bonds as well.

5. December 31st. This is "cliff" deadline which I have written about in other places on this site. Up for action are the tax breaks for the rich, taxes on the middle class, cuts for the military, and other bread and butter items.

No telling what will happen. Uncertainty can really trigger ancillary events, most unpleasant.

But what should the average citizen do about the above situations? Stay tuned.

But first to be clear about what the average citizen is up against. School is out-here; you and I have to be clear that the monied classes do not have your and my best interests at heart. Here is what I mean.

To be clear:

1. Banks, corporations and wall street love high unemployment- which means people are desperate and work for half wages-this has happened already.
2. They love recession because prices fall down drastically and since they have all of our money, have kicked us out of our homes, they have the cash and buy up these cheap homes themselves at half prices. Most foreclosed

properties are bought by the banks themselves, and the down-priced homes also now have lower taxes.

3- They love war since war profiteers get rich and to boot they have made many communities in the US dependent upon the local war industries dependent upon them and the Pentagon for jobs.

4. They love privatizing schools and have attacked the public school system, depriving the schools of revenue and tax money and then come in saying the schools are failing and should be privatized into "charter" and for profit schools owned by them.

5. They love drugs and crime and fill up the jails with people of color in a new Jim Crow system and, in addition, this provides jobs in rural communities run by private companies. The industrial prison complex is a jobs program for rural constituencies and well as billions for farmers--all wall street republicans.

6. They make billions off school loans and even the school lunch programs is run by JP Morgan Chase for *profit*.

See what I mean. I could go on.

But on tomorrow let's get back to what can be done to put all this back on track a sustainable track.

Possible triggers of financial trouble?
Five more triggers set to fizzle or ignite in the next six days on wall street, the banks and JP Morgan--one pundits view.

We will throw these into the mix and get back our analysis tomorrow.

9/11/12

Well where are we in the never-ending European Debt Crisis and what is likely to happen?

First, there is a clear anti-Merkel trend. Socialists have won elections or gained strength in France, possibility Holland, in Italy, now it looks Spain is rebelling against austerity as well.

Second, the European Central bank while offering unlimited funds may find that nobody wants those funds with the conditions now attached and the fact of the matter is that more debt cannot cure existing debt.

If that happens what will happen? The possibilities and outcomes:

1. Rolling default. Country after country may opt out of the zone or threaten to do so-getting concessions on the austerity plans-- which it is clear, stifle growth.
The Germans would lose. Yes, the Germans would lose because they sell many if not most of their products to the PIIGs. Inflation would occur
and the creditor nations would lose and take the haircut, even if the zone fell apart. After all, the Greeks reason, austerity and default start to look alike except default

regains Greek sovereignty and that looks good to Greeks and the other nations right now.

2. Expect a planned default- with reverberations in the United States as well. That is why President Obama is promising an increase in exports. He plans to let the US currency float thereby increasing exports. He has to to put some Americans back to work. A cheap dollar helps.

3. Meantime the Chinese and the Russians see this coming as well and are talking now about creating trade and currency agreements between themselves which would insulate them from the dollar and its collapse.

They are even talking commodity trades not based on currency but a form of barter. And that could work, and if it does, other nations could start to imitate it--trouble for the west.

JP Morgan and municipalities

http://www.businessweek.com/news/2012-09-13/detroit-shows-wall-street-never-loses-on-bad-swaps-muni-credit

Other factors:
http://www.bbc.co.uk/news/world-19431890

  http://www.reuters.com/article/2012/09/16/us-usa-fed-economy-idUSBRE88F05A20120916

9/28/12

Trends in the ECM
France to tax the rich and down play austerity--a trend to

go worldwide? Will this work in the US. Yes, apparently, this author says.

http://www.nationofchange.org/add-it-taxes-avoided-rich-could-pay-deficit-1346074084

http://www.bbc.co.uk/news/world-europe-19755417

http://www.bbc.co.uk/news/world-europe-19754016

9/28/12

Who works less, goes to school fewer hours, and is most productive in the world and avoided recession? Guess who?

http://www.bbc.co.uk/news/business-18868704

Bush tax cuts caused the deficit?

http://www.businessweek.com/articles/2012-08-02/the-fiscal-cliff-we-all-saw-coming#r=shared

9/29/12 German, France support financial transactions tax

http://www.nytimes.com/2012/09/29/business/global/germany-and-france-join-to-support-tax-on-financial-trades.html?partner=rss&emc=rss

9/29/12 What was the Great Depression like?

http://topics.nytimes.com/top/reference/timestopics/subject

s/g/great_depression_1930s/index.html?inline=nyt-classifier

9/29/12

How has QE3 gone so far?

http://www.businessinsider.com/think-bernanke-2012-9

10/1/12

Will reform or jail offered to bankers work in England and spread to the US. No doubt we will be impacted if this occurs because rules set in London will have global impact.

http://www.independent.co.uk/news/uk/home-news/bad-bankers-warned-repent-or-go-to-jail-8191493.html

http://www.independent.co.uk/news/business/news/burnt-in-effigy-martin-wheatley-has-the-steel-to-shake-city-8191496.html

11/19/12

What is the end game of the monied classes--buying up cheap assets
and privatizing the world?

http://www.nytimes.com/2012/11/18/business/privatizing-greece-slowly-but-not-surely.html?partner=rss&emc=rss&_r=0

11/9/12 Debt as a means of control

The Debt Resistors Manual

http://strikedebt.org/The-Debt-Resistors-Operations-Manual.pdf

11/25/12

The World Shadow Banking System-How it Works.

http://www.youtube.com/watch?feature=player_detailpage&v=XliTvxqTtsE

What are the issues in the fiscal Cliff? Video

http://www.youtube.com/watch?feature=player_detailpage&v=Ra-VsLwbW2c

12/17/17

http://www.cbsnews.com/8301-34222_162-57559699-10391739/obama-moves-on-taxes-in-latest-cliff-counter-proposal/

http://www.cnn.com/2012/12/17/politics/fiscal-cliff/

http://www.washingtonpost.com/politics/obama-boehner-meet-as-debt-talks-intensify/2012/12/17/6b43c24a-4868-11e2-b6f0-e851e741d196_story.html

12/19/12

http://truth-out.org/opinion/item/13401-fiscal-cliff-fiscal-cliff-lets-call-their-bluff#13559566899431&action=collapse_widget&id=3621285

http://thehill.com/blogs/on-the-money/domestic-taxes/273421-boehner-moves-to-plan-b

http://abcnews.go.com/blogs/politics/2012/12/liberals-bash-obamas-fiscal-cliff-offer/

http://www.cbsnews.com/8301-18563_162-57559900/boehner-unveils-plan-b-as-fiscal-cliff-deadline-looms/

So, we might ask, what is wrong with Obama's offer to the republicans?

First, it puts social security one the table after he ran on a platform of refusing any cuts to social security. This is a republican goal which he, Obama, is now offering to them free of charge.

Cuts to the rate of future benefit growth is a cut no matter how you try to explain it away and, most importantly, puts future cuts and adjustments on the table for the entire safety net.

Ditto for Medicaid and Medicare.

Medical costs and drug costs are double in this country

compared to other countries and that is solely because republicans have placed the health care system inside the for-profit gouging private sector. Take it out of privatization and our costs drop drastically.

All of this is the slippery slope and the mirage of a "fiscal cliff" helps sell the changes the republicans want and have wanted for decades.

And what does Obama get back for these concessions in the republican Plan B?--tax cuts which essentially leave income and special tax deductions in place for the rich, increases in payroll taxes for the middle class, leaves the unemployed with no money as of January 1, 2013 and Obama goes away with nothing in return. That is the essence of Plan B.

Should be called Plan BS.

Who wins here? Wall street wins again because just after a cut in the benefits for social security wall street we will be writing recipients telling them that they can make up for the cuts if they just allow a portion of their checks to be "invested" in a special social security fund wall street is setting up just for them.

This will be described as "voluntary" when in fact it will not be.

Social security is not part of any deficit at all but is being thrust forward because wall street wants to get it hands on the social security fund, the only large pot of government money it does not currently control.

So social security's older people will be made to pay for the wall street bailout disaster. There ain't no justice.

12/20/12

http://thehill.com/homenews/senate/274009-reid-rules-out-senate-vote-on-boehners-plan-b

12/20/12
Only one of the two "Plan B" bill passed. What does it all mean? See below.

http://thehill.com/homenews/house/274187-house-gop-pulls-plan-b

http://www.cbsnews.com/8301-250_162-57559974/the-middle-class-tax-hikes-in-obamas-fiscal-cliff-plan/

Even CBS questions whether there is a Fiscal Cliff.

http://www.cbsnews.com/8301-250_162-57554264/the-fiscal-cliff-isnt-a-cliff-at-all/

And yet other views.

http://www.weeklystandard.com/articles/real-cliff_666593.html

http://money.msn.com/business-news/article.aspx?feed=OBR&date=20121220&id=15777069

http://www.huffingtonpost.com/ethan-rome/boehners-plan-b-is-all-bu_b_2331593.html

12/20/12 The proposed budget cuts no one is talking about.

http://www.thestreet.com/story/11798889/1/here-are-the-budget-cuts-president-obama-has-offered.html

12/27/12
Who has gotten what share of the profits between corporations, management and labor over the years?

http://www.pbs.org/newshour/rundown/2012/12/capital-wins-labor-loses-but-andrew-smithers-says-it-cant-go-on.html

12/28/12

What the provisions of Obama Care are due to come into effect in 2013 which will affect you? Several.

http://thehill.com/blogs/healthwatch/health-reform-implementation/274693-five-obamacare-provisions-to-watch-in-2013

http://blogs.voanews.com/breaking-news/2012/12/28/us-senate-votes-to-extend-warrantless-surveillance-act/

12/28/12

American Civil Liberties take it on the chin

http://blogs.voanews.com/breaking-news/2012/12/28/us-senate-votes-to-extend-warrantless-surveillance-act/

12/30/12

What is going on inside Fiscal Cliff negotiations? The report today, Sunday December 30, 2012. What is the latest?

http://thehill.com/homenews/senate/274909-reid-and-mcconnell-fail-to-reach-agreement-to-avoid-fiscal-cliff

http://thehill.com/homenews/senate/274917-mcconnell-talking-to-biden-willing-to-drop-social-security-demand

Interesting site on Occupy Wall Street and the FBI

http://www.economicpopulist.org/content/occupy-wall-street-labeled-terrorists-fbi

12/31/12

What are the outlines of the latest Fiscal Cliff Deal?

See the long quote below from the Dec 31st LA Times

"Both parties were under enormous pressure from their political bases not to give in to what some, including Sen. Tom Harkin (D-Iowa), a liberal leader, characterized as simply a "bad deal."

More than $660 billion in revenue would be raised – far less than the target Obama first set in talks with congressional leaders. The president sought $1.6 trillion in new revenue from a large deficit-reduction package, and at least $800 billion in earlier talks with Republicans over a deal on tax increases.

The agreement would set the top tax rates at 39.6% for income above $450,000 for households and $400,000 for individuals, which is a narrower definition of who is wealthy than Obama once sought, according to a source who was not authorized to discuss the negotiations. The president won reelection campaigning on asking those who earn above $250,000 to contribute more in taxes.

Investment income tax rates would also rise for those higher-income households, from the historic low 15% rate on capital gains and dividends to a new 20% rate. The president had sought to tax dividends at the same rate as ordinary income, and his earlier offer sought to initiate those taxes at the lower $250,000 income threshold.

The estate tax, which has been a key sticking point throughout the weekend of negotiations, appears to have been settled. The agreement splits the difference, setting the new rate at 40% on estates valued at more than $5 million – a compromise between today's 35% rate and the 45% rate Democrats sought on estates of $3.5 million or more.

Americans would benefit from an extension of long-term unemployment benefits, which expired over the weekend, for one full year.

One area that hewed closer to Democratic priorities was Obama's proposal to reinstate the phase-out of personal exemption tax credits and itemized deductions on upper-income households. They had been in place before the George W. Bush-era tax cuts began in 2001, but were done away with over the past decade and would fully expire, with the rest of the tax breaks, on New Year's Eve."

More in the last few minutes"

http://www.guardian.co.uk/world/2012/dec/31/fiscal-cliff-congress-deadline-live#block-50e2037a95cb94a7be21b5da

Obama Caves? Apparently

http://www.washingtonpost.com/business/fiscal-cliff/biden-mcconnell-continue-cliff-talks-as-clock-winds-down/2012/12/31/66c044e2-534d-11e2-8b9e-dd8773594efc_story.html

1/1/13

http://www.washingtonpost.com/politics/after-a-fiscal-cliff-deal-what-next/2012/12/31/b9d9a452-5384-11e2-bf3e-76c0a789346f_story.html

What happened in the House Vote for the Fiscal Cliff?

http://thehill.com/homenews/senate/275101-senate-fiscal-cliff-deal-in-trouble-in-house

My predictions for World trends in 2013-2014 in various areas.

Let's have a look in the following areas as to what the future is likely to bring in the United States and globally. In the coming days we will go through my thoughts and predications in a variety of areas.
(If you want back-ground on my previous predictions and how accurate they have or have not been, I suggest you read first my blog on this site entitled "My Report Card on Obama" and "What America Needs to Do to Survive" also on this site.

After the Fiscal Cliff-What?
The arrangement, now completed, is only temporary.

The phony Washington-made Fiscal Cliff will continue in even a more heated fashion in the next three months where the issues and the deadlock battles will continue over:

1-R*aising the National Debt Ceiling. Due up in February*
The republicans are promising a war over this.

2-*Reducing Expenditures and Raising more Revenue.* The Cliff bill basically punted these issues down the road, kicking the can, so to speak. But in two months we will not be able to kick the can because we will need to save our canned goods for a rainy day.

Obama did not do a good job on the level of:
    a. He did not avert a middle class tax increase in the

payroll taxes most Americans pay each month. Up from 4 percent to 6.2 percent. This is a pocket book issue and hurts poor families the most and, most importantly, hurts the economy because they and businesses will now not spend that money. (Remember businesses pay half of these taxes and employees pay the other half.)

b. Medicare taxes are also part of payroll taxes and **ouch**.

c. He told us he needed 1.6 trillion in new tax revenue to help with the deficit and he, in this Cliff deal, got only 660 billion. So where will the rest of the money come from? The rich will say "not us" "we had our taxes raised in the Cliff deal so the middle class will have to make up the difference this time."

So one can look at the Cliff deal as one where Obama lost more than he got or sought and the difference or 1 trillion dollars-will likely have to be paid by the middle class at this date and there is no real plan about what to do to avoid this unhappy outcome.

Real anger will arise when people realize what has happened. This was done as many of the corporate and wall street free handouts were continued.

See article below:
http://www.alternet.org/news-amp-politics/8-huge-corporate-handouts-fiscal-cliff-bill?akid=9885.260128.O3TgRh&rd=1&src=newsletter769711&t=4

d. Most of the Republicans now can run in 2014 on their favorite grounds- spending cuts must now "balance the budget" while Obama looks like he is advocating more "spending" and looks like a tax and spend democrat. This is a losing move for a democrat in the year before the 2014 Congressional elections.

e. The second part of this tri-feta is the upcoming battle in April-May over the Appropriations bills. These bills are the spending bills for the government for 2013-2014.

In Washington it is one thing to pass a law but just you try and get that law funded and the republicans many times refuse to fund a bill that they voted for. This includes the entire budget of the US Government and to boot they will for sure refuse to vote to increase the debt ceiling for bills they voted for in the first place. This is tantamount to default and the US will be seen in default because the expenditures include not just social programs, the military and the like ,but also, debt we owe to the American people, bonds and the like but to other countries who have loaned us money and the billions owed the banks.

The interest "owed" these criminal banks who loaned the Federal government our money, our daily deposits. mind you, comes to 450 billion a year.

This "debt" is phony in the extreme, is almost the size of the military budget of the United States (500-600 billion estimated) and is basically credit card debt run up to pay for the Bush Billionaire tax cuts, two wars, and the bail out of the banks. So us tax payers have to pay the bill on all this while, if there are any profits, the banks keep those profits? This makes no sense what so ever and is privatized profits for the rich and socialized losses paid for by the middle class and the poor.

    f. A trigger point will be in April when the tax revenue for the Federal government will become clear and now clearly with this Cliff deal they will be short. Will less revenue than planned for the US government will fall once again into the bank debt trap where the Federal Reserve will have to loan still more money to the government (our money by the way) and the cycle spirals toward bust. And not the Federal Reserve is continuing the bail out of the banks to the tune of 85 billion dollars a month! This on top of that will likely create another fiscal crisis.

A last note on debt:

The World GNP is 70 trillion a year.

The US deficit is about 1.6 trillion.

The derivative debt the banks are holding and hiding is close to a quadrillion dollars including the hedge funds.

Therefore, our World Income is only 70 trillion a year and our World Debt is a thousand trillion.

What is wrong with this picture?

Quote:
"It would be hard to overstate the recklessness of these

banks. The numbers that you are about to see are absolutely jaw-dropping. According to <u>the Comptroller of the Currency</u>, four of the largest U.S. banks are walking a tightrope of risk, leverage and debt when it comes to derivatives. Just check out how exposed they are...

JPMorgan Chase

Total Assets: $1,812,837,000,000 (just over 1.8 trillion dollars)

Total Exposure To Derivatives: $69,238,349,000,000 (more than 69 trillion dollars)

Citibank

Total Assets: $1,347,841,000,000 (a bit more than 1.3 trillion dollars)

Total Exposure To Derivatives: $52,150,970,000,000 (more than 52 trillion dollars)

Bank Of America

Total Assets: $1,445,093,000,000 (a bit more than 1.4 trillion dollars)

Total Exposure To Derivatives: $44,405,372,000,000 (more than 44 trillion dollars)

Goldman Sachs

Total Assets: $114,693,000,000 (a bit more than 114 billion dollars - yes, you read that correctly)

Total Exposure To Derivatives: $41,580,395,000,000 (more than 41 trillion dollars)

That means that the total exposure that Goldman Sachs has to derivatives contracts is **more than 362 times greater** than their total assets.

To get a better idea of the massive amounts of money that we are talking about, just check out this excellent infographic."

So what does a trillion dollars look like? http://demonocracy.info/infographics/usa/derivatives/bank exposure.html

Golly.

What is wrong is that there is no way we will ever pay that debt and all of world politics and economic maneuverings are essentially the rich, wall streets, and the Central banks of the world who lost that money in a global Ponzi scheme trying to force the middle classes of the world to pay off the debt and losses they ran up but forcing the middle classes of the world into taxing themselves into poverty to pay for it while the rich preserve their wealth.

1/6/13

Spelling out how Banks and the finance sector use debt as a means of controlling all of society.

http://truth-out.org/news/item/13718-the-financial-war-against-the-economy-at-large

That friends is what is going on and constitutes the major financial driver globally speaking--all going by the name of "austerity."

So, the gross driver is now identified, tomorrow, and in the coming days, we will begin to look at what will happen in 2013-2014 in the following areas:

1- Politics
2- Global and US Markets
3- Energy
4- Food
5- Climate Driven Changes
6- Unemployment

One pundits view
http://theeconomiccollapseblog.com/archives/unemployment-is-not-going-down-the-employment-rate-has-been-under-59-percent-for-39-months-in-a-row

7- Your Pension, Bonds and 2013
8- Currency Wars
(See videos-articles below for differing views and predictions)

http://www.youtube.com/watch?feature=player_detailpage&v=LRPCTrSDaqY

http://www.telegraph.co.uk/finance/comment/ambroseevan

s_pritchard/9773911/Stocks-to-soar-as-world-money-catches-fire-Calvinst-Europe-left-behind.html

See you tomorrow.

1/6/13

The true history of the ball outs and after.

http://www.rollingstone.com/politics/news/secret-and-lies-of-the-bailout-20130104?print=true

4/18/13

What bailouts and low and negative interest rates mean for seniors.

They are robbed of their retirement and their life savings.

http://www.washingtonpost.com/business/economy/low-interest-rate-environment-expose-seniors-to-fraudsters/2013/04/18/63d065dc-9c77-11e2-a941-a19bce7af755_story.html

5/4/13

Obama offering up cuts to Medicare? Say it isn't so.

http://www.kaiserhealthnews.org/Daily-Reports/2013/May/03/budget-issues.aspx

5/5/13

Apple profits offshore could fund the sequester?

at: http://www.truth-out.org/opinion/item/16177-apple-dodges-enough-taxes-to-cover-much-of-the-sequester

5/6/13

Banks getting sued over failure to follow through on mortgage settlement.

http://dealbook.nytimes.com/2013/05/06/new-york-to-sue-bank-of-america-and-wells-fargo-over-settlement-violations/

Ideas some people are putting forth to opt out of the jaws of Wall Street.

http://www.truth-out.org/news/item/16233-opting-out-of-wall-street-and-building-sustainable-resilient-communities-remaking-finance-part-iii

5/10/13

Social Security--What you need to know about who is getting screwed.

http://truth-out.org/news/item/16213-social-securitys-explosive-injustices

5/20/13

http://thehill.com/blogs/on-the-money/banking-financial-institutions/300531-senators-want-to-move-forward-with-fannie-freddie-reform

5/21/13

Dimon beats back stockholder revolt

http://www.bbc.co.uk/news/business-22618381

5/23/13
The IRS scandal governed by politics?

http://www.motherjones.com/politics/2013/05/congress-irs-tea-party-gift-tax-donor?google_editors_picks=true

5/24/13

http://dealbook.nytimes.com/2013/05/23/banks-lobbyists-help-in-drafting-financial-bills/

5/24/13

Who Voted to keep JP Morgan Chief in his dual roles and why?

http://www.economist.com/news/finance-and-economics/21578392-banks-shareholders-prefer-keep-devil-they-know-unbreakable-dimon

5/26/13

Wall Street Tries to Kill Financial Reform

http://www.delawareonline.com/apps/pbcs.dll/article?AID=/201305260910/BUSINESS05/305260059

http://www.globalresearch.ca/banks-own-the-us-government/14214

http://www.globalresearch.ca/who-calls-the-shots-government-of-by-and-for-the-banks/5336430

6/1/13

Confiscation of depositors accounts-the new normal? Time for public banks-get rid of the private banks?

http://webofdebt.wordpress.com/

Time to get rid of the federal reserve bank which is not federal, not governmental, but is run and owned by the major banks in this country.

http://moneymorning.com/2013/05/28/do-we-really-need-the-federal-reserve-system/

Below find great radio show on debt and banks role in all of this: Radio show-available for download only three weeks.

Wait until the gospel music is over and the first segment on a local protest. Then the debt part of the program begins. Debt show begins in at about 35 minutes into the show. Worth looking for it.

http://www.kpfa.org/archive/id/92093

 -Five things you didn't know about the true nature of the Federal Reserve Bank

http://moneymorning.com/2013/05/08/5-things-the-federal-reserve-hopes-youll-never-find-out/moneymorning.com/2013/05/08/5-things-the-federal-reserve-hopes-youll-never-find-out/

More radio shows on the Fed, Banks and the Public bank option\
http://www.kpfa.org/archive/show/34

The World Banking System described as "corrupt" by a former insider:

http://www.thenewamerican.com/economy/economics/item/15473-world-bank-insider-blows-whistle-on-corruption-federal-reserve

Scathing Critique of the Federal Reserve Bank

http://www.forbes.com/sites/shahgilani/2013/05/31/fix-america-fire-the-fed/

6/4/13
The notion of economy and its history. Money as symbolic exchange and not based on anything real.

http://www.kpfa.org/archive/id/92180

"With the relaxation of the laws against usury in early modern Europe, money became an autonomous power, acquiring its own interests and making its own demands, as if it were alive. Money behaves like a living creature when it takes on the definitive characteristic of life: the ability to reproduce. But money is not part of the natural universe. No one can touch or taste a piece of financial value. Money is merely a sign representing alienated human life, and "capitalism" is the name we give to the process of our own objectification."

Hawkes Critique of Norm Chomsky at:

http://www.the-tls.co.uk/tls/public/article1114177.ece

Wage Slaves and Capitalism

http://emc.eserver.org/1-4/hawkes.html

6/5/13

Wall Street and the small investor.

"When it comes to Wall Street profitability the most lucrative transactions are not coming from servicing *"Mom and Pop"* retail clients trying to work their way towards retirement. Wall Street is not "invested" along with you but rather use you to make income. This is why "buy and hold" investment strategies are so widely promoted. As long as your dollars are invested the mutual funds and brokerage firms collect fees regardless of market conditions. While *"buy and hold"* strategies are certainly in their best interest - it is not necessarily yours. However, these fees are a byline to the really big money.

In reality, Wall Street is focused on the multi-million, and billion, dollar investment banking transactions, such as public offerings, mergers, acquisitions and bond offerings which generate hundreds of millions to billions of dollars in fees for Wall Street each year."

Read more:

http://www.streettalklive.com/daily-x-change/1716-the-truth-about-wall-street-analysts-why-you-need-independence.html#ixzz2VO91qlU1

Welfare for the Wealthy?
http://opinionator.blogs.nytimes.com/2013/06/04/welfare-for-the-wealthy/

 6/7/13

One pundit's predictions for what will happen in 2014 in the finance world:

"The Painful Price of Subsidized Money"

http://moneymorning.com/2013/06/07/the-painful-price-of-subsidized-money/

6/10/13

How Tech companies and Wall Street who financed them have stolen the future of youth worldwide.

http://www.nationofchange.org/how-tech-companies-are-cheating-america-s-young-adults-1370878407

Bank profits soar while wages stagnate. Who is getting the profits?

http://truth-out.org/news/item/16879-bank-profits-soar-wages-suffer-sharpest-decline-in-60-years

6/12/13
Where have the jobs gone?

Where have the jobs gone?
MIT study on that subject.

http://www.technologyreview.com/featuredstory/515926/how-technology-is-destroying-jobs/

6/14/13

Obama caves in to Wall Street again. Derivatives to remain unregulated?

http://www.forbes.com/sites/robertlenzner/2013/06/14/obama-rewards-wall-street-again-thwarts-reform-by-sacking-gensler/

http://www.bloomberg.com/news/2013-06-12/inflation-at-53-year-low-belies-u-s-demand-strength-economy.html

http://moneymorning.com/2013/06/18/obama-sells-us-down-the-river-again/

6/17/13

Why has no single wall street executive been prosecuted and gone to jail?

http://www.pbs.org/wgbh/pages/frontline/business-economy-financial-crisis/untouchables/is-wall-street-still-untouchable/

Wall street eyes Africa as the next boom continent? Run Africa.

http://www.bbc.co.uk/news/world-africa-22847118

6/19/13

Former Bank of America employees sue claiming Bank of America told them to lie about foreclosures.

http://blog.al.com/wire/2013/06/former_bank_of_america_employe.html

http://www.salon.com/2013/06/18/check_out_the_full_bank_of_america_whistleblower_details_affidavits/singleton/

6/19/13

America's middle class slowly sinking, ranked 27th in the world

http://www.alternet.org/economy/americas-middle-class-27thrichest?akid=10589.260128.Z0jdvx&rd=1&src=newsletter 857124&t=4

6/19/13

The Eminent Domain Movement Comes to California

http://www.authorsden.com/visit/viewshortstory.asp?id=56 607&authorid=121255

6/20/13

How banks have not lived up to mortgage agreement with homeowners

http://online.wsj.com/article/SB100014241278873233000 04578555141517583344.html

Banking report out in England. Recommends jailing bankers and more:

http://m.guardiannews.com/commentisfree/joris-luyendijk-banking-blog/2013/jun/19/banking-britain-beyond-control

9/21/13

Supreme Court sides with Corporations against consumer

http://mobile.bloomberg.com/news/2013-06-21/consumer-loans-insulated-from-fed-even-as-mortgages-rise.html

http://m.motherjones.com/politics/2013/06/consumers-get-screwed-scotus-american-express-decision-small-biz

9/22/13

85 billion a month being given to the banks soon to stop?

"Five years since the 2008 financial meltdown, the speculation and fraud that caused the crash are back in full force in the United States. Flush with the $85 billion in cash printed up and handed to the banks every month by the Federal Reserve, business at the Wall Street casino is booming. Stock values are at record levels and so are bank profits, amidst declining wages and mass poverty."

http://www.globalresearch.ca/who-calls-the-shots-government-of-by-and-for-the-banks/5336430

Bernanke just hints that the 85 billion a month might end in 6 months to a year and the stock market plunges 500 points in three days.

Why should this be so?
Let's explore this in the coming days looking at the down on the ground relationship between the Federal Reserve's 85 billion a month give-away to the banks and the levels of the stock market.

First think about this way, if I gave you 85 billion a month, and you are an American bank, what do they do with it?

Here are a few first answers.

1. Banks don't lend it to Americans seeking loans. They see Americans as too old, losing their purchasing power, maxed out on their credit cards, student debt at a trillion dollars and have concluded that it is bad business to give

Americans loans. So they loan it overseas where there is cheap labor and have abandoned Americans in what some have called 'economic treason." They take our money after we have given them infrastructure and government guarantees and gives that money to others. If they fail in these "investments" the US government bails them out. Honest this really happens.

2. They also gamble with that money on derivatives. Most American's don't know that a stock broker can by a stock with just 10% down hoping that is 30, 60 or 90 days that the stock will rise. Some say they fix the market so a given stock will rise or fall based on their bets. So banks gamble with each other and other foreign banks with these bets. They take out in addition, insurance policies on both sides of a given bet, just like Las Vegas.

More tomorrow.

6/22/13

Bank stocks sink like a stone.

http://www.fool.com/investing/general/2013/06/21/why-jpmorgan-sank-like-a-stone-this-week.aspx

Sink because the gambling money is going to get cut off.

Who or what is ALEC?

http://www.nationofchange.org/united-states-alec-privatizing-america-one-statehouse-time-1371908974

6/24/13

76% of American living pay-check to pay-check?

http://money.cnn.com/2013/06/24/pf/emergency-savings/index.html?iid=s_mpm

 What does it mean for your mortgage? Conservative Senators propose to end them and give mortgages to the private sector.

http://www.washingtonpost.com/business/economy/senators-introduce-bipartisan-bill-to-replace-fannie-freddie-with-new-agency/2013/06/25/c5437850-dd9e-11e2-b197-f248b21f94c4_story.html

6/26/13

The Bond Market is on the brink of collapse. What does it mean?

See link on this page. It will affect you and me, not next year but in a few weeks-in fact it is already under way.

http://www.bloomberg.com/news/2013-06-26/u-s-bond-funds-have-record-61-7-billion-in-redemptions.html
See:

http://www.authorsden.com/visit/viewshortstory.asp?AuthorID=121255&id=59045

 World finances which lead to rebellion"
Fuel, food and housing and jobs

6/28/13

Africa as the next colonization target.

http://www.nationofchange.org/commercial-colonisation-africa-1372434364

6/28/13

How did we get to this crisis point? One point of view.

http://www.speakingtree.in/spiritual-blogs/masters/philosophy/the-occupy-wall-street-movement-demise-of-crony-capitalism

6/28/13

As predicted Mortgage rates rise at record pace.

http://www.foxbusiness.com/personal-finance/2013/06/28/rising-mortgage-rates-straw-that-breaks-recovery-back/

http://www.foxbusiness.com/personal-finance/2013/06/27/wow-mortgages-jump-almost-half-percent/?intcmp=trending

6/29/13

Gold falls to new three year low. What does it mean?

"The shine has come off gold since the precious metal hit highs of $1,895 an ounce in 2011, buoyed by its status as a safe haven for investors. Over the last fortnight prices have dropped by around 15% – the steepest fall in 30 years –

largely driven by a strong signal from the chairman of the Federal Reserve, Ben Bernanke, is that he intends to cut back the US central bank's $85bn-a-month stimulus program."

http://www.guardian.co.uk/business/2013/jun/28/gold-price-low-federal-reserve-inflation

Mortgage hit 26 year high?

http://www.staradvertiser.com/news/breaking/213322471.html?id=213322471

6/30/13

Too big to fail major banks will not be able to survive a financial shock- say regulators

"An increasingly vocal chorus of current and former U.S. regulators says the biggest banks still have not provided adequate plans to safely wind down in bankruptcy and may need to be restructured to reduce the risk they pose to the financial system.

Jim Wigand, a Federal Deposit Insurance Corp. official responsible for planning for the failures of big banks such as JPMorgan Chase, Goldman Sachs and Citigroup, said none have yet been able to draw up bankruptcy plans that wouldn't threaten to detonate the financial system"

From:

http://www.journalnow.com/business/business_news/natio

nal_international/article_f9cc9c1e-e118-11e2-8d2f-001a4bcf6878.html

7/1/13

The US middle class ranked lowest in the world, just in front of Russia.

http://www.nationofchange.org/more-evidence-our-middle-class-sliding-toward-third-world-1372686156

And is there a war on the unemployed?

http://www.nytimes.com/2013/07/01/opinion/krugman-the-war-on-the-unemployed.html?src=un&feedurl=http%3A%2F%2Fjson8.nytimes.com%2Fpages%2Fopinion%2Findex.jsonp

7/3/13

New Federal Reserve Rules for capital requirement for banks. Good for the middle class or bad for the middle class?

https://mail.google.com/mail/u/0/h/pzzxze2ev4mt/?&v=c&th=13fa5c605949c16c

7/3/13
Big banks to be investigated by EU authorities for 2008 behavior.

"This statement of objections is a formal step in EU investigations that charges the banks, the dealers' association, and the swaps pricing agent and index controller of "colluding to prevent exchanges from entering the credit derivatives business between 2006 and 2009."

The companies are then expected to answer the charges.

"If, after the parties have exercised their rights of defense, the Commission concludes that there is sufficient evidence of an infringement, it can issue a decision prohibiting the conduct and impose a fine of up to 10% of a company's annual worldwide turnover.""

"In a press release Monday the European Commission announced it sent a "statement of objections" to **Bank of America Merrill Lynch (BAC), Barclays (BARC)**, Bear Stearns , **BNP Paribas (BNP), Citigroup (C),** Credit **Suisse (CS), Deutsche Bank (DB), Goldman Sachs (GS), HSBC (HBC), JP Morgan (JPM), Morgan Stanley (MS), Royal Bank of Scotland (RBS), UBS (UBS)** as well as the International Swaps and Derivatives Association (ISDA) and data service provider Markit."

From:

http://moneymorning.com/2013/07/03/the-big-banks-on-trial-again/

http://rt.com/shows/keiser-report/episode-466-max-keiser-651/

7/5/13

Black teen unemployment rate at 95%. This is a bomb waiting to explode.

http://www.pbs.org/newshour/businessdesk/2013/07/jobless-rate-for-poor-black-te.html

This is no accident. Now employment equals crime and drop outs which equal early contact with the criminal justice system and tracking these kids into prison so for-profit prison owners have a steady supply of prisoners and keep those cells filled since they are paid by the number of beds filled. This is cash for kids.

7/6/13

The Demographic Time bomb facing all of Europe, China, Japan and Russia and the United States.

http://moneymorning.com/2013/07/01/big-problems-these-countries-are-facing-demographic-time-bombs/

More on this later.

7/8/13

EU oks taking money directly from consumer bank accounts

http://www.truth-out.org/news/item/17433-think-your-money-is-safe-in-an-insured-bank-account-think-again

"WASHINGTON -- The nation's eight largest banks would have to meet tougher leverage limits than required under international standards as part of new rules proposed Tuesday by federal regulators designed to protect taxpayers from another financial crisis.

Under the plan, Bank of America Corp., JP Morgan Chase & Co., Citigroup Inc. and the five other U.S. bank holding companies designated as "systemically important financial institutions" would have to hold capital equal to at least 5% of their total assets.

The federally insured banks owned by those companies, such as Citibank and Chase bank, would have to hold capital equal to at least 6% of their assets, according to the proposed rules.

Other U.S. banks and bank holding companies only have to meet a 3% leverage ratio under rules adopted by regulators as part of an international agreement known as Basel 3."

"The extra capital for the largest banks is designed to protect the Federal Deposit Insurance Corp. fund that covers most deposits when an institution fails.

It also is designed to protect taxpayers who might be on the hook for losses if one of the largest banks has to be seized and dismantled by regulators to prevent damage to the financial system and broader economy.

As of the third quarter of 2012, the eight bank holding companies would need to increase their capital by a combined $63 billion to meet a 5% leverage ratio, regulators said. The banking units of those companies would have to raise a combined $89 billion in capital to meet their proposed 6% leverage ratio.

Banks that didn't meet the new ratios would face restrictions on dividend payments, stock buybacks and executive bonus payments, according to the rules proposed by the FDIC, the Federal Reserve and the Office of the Comptroller of the Currency."

From:

http://touch.latimes.com/#section/1780/article/p2p-76607101/

But what we want to know is what does this finance-speak means for you and me?

Let's look tomorrow.

7/9/13

Market rigging? NY Attorney General begins inquiry

http://dealbook.nytimes.com/2013/07/08/regulators-examining-sales-of-early-financial-data/

The Regular of Fannie Mae and Freddie Mac under the gun and being sued for blocking payments to low income housing groups.

http://www.reuters.com/article/2013/07/09/us-usa-housing-lawsuit-idUSBRE96810520130709

7/10/13

Inside JP Morgan Bank

http://www.alternet.org/economy/jp-morgan-chase-bank-4-trillion-global-powerhouse-meet-elites-charge?akid=10674.260128.LWsWDw&rd=1&src=newsletter866634&t=6&paging=off

Video history of plutocracy

http://www.youtube.com/watch?feature=player_detailpage&v=YdYqDV6_BP8

The real jobs situation in this country.

"As David Stockman has noted, the U.S. economy has only regained 200,000 of the **5.6 million** breadwinner jobs that were lost during the last recession...

By September 2012, the S&P 500 was up by 115 percent from its recession lows and had recovered all of its losses from the peak of the second Greenspan bubble. By contrast, only 200,000 of the 5.6 million lost breadwinner jobs had been recovered by that same point in time. To be sure, the Fed's Wall Street shills breathlessly reported the improved jobs "print" every month, picking and choosing starting and ending points and using continuously revised and seasonally maladjusted data to support that illusion. Yet the fundamentals with respect to breadwinner jobs could not be obfuscated."

From:

https://mail.google.com/mail/h/12g8366415d91/?&v=c&th=13fc79a977781695

7/11/13

The Fed gave away 13 trillion dollars in 2008-9 and still giving away 85 billion of our money today. Why?

http://news.goldseek.com/GoldSeek/1347653228.php

http://timesofindia.indiatimes.com/world/us/US-govt-reports-116-5-billion-surplus-in-June/articleshow/21027655.cms

7/11/13
Senators introduce bills to curb wall street

http://dealbook.nytimes.com/2013/07/11/senators-introduce-bill-to-separate-trading-activities-from-big-banks/

http://www.bloomberg.com/news/2013-07-11/warren-joins-mccain-to-push-new-glass-steagall-bill-for-banks.html

7/12/13

http://thehill.com/blogs/regwatch/finance/310489-cftceuropeans-reach-deal-for-international-swaps

7/13/13

Will McCain and Warren get a new Glass-Steagall bill through? Maybe or maybe not.

http://www.huffingtonpost.com/2013/07/12/jpmorgan-chase-glass-steagall_n_3587062.html

Warren fights

http://www.nbcnews.com/id/45755883/ns/msnbc-the_last_word/vp/52495072#52495136

7/18/13

Supreme Court Millionaires. Who influences them?

http://rt.com/usa/justice-alito-financial-report-millions-236/

7/20/13
Elizabeth Warren ruffling feathers in the Senate. Yea, Elizabeth

http://thehill.com/homenews/senate/312397-elizabeth-warren-ruffling-feathers-early-in-clubby-senate

7/20/13

Most people start spacing out if you mention commodity

trading considering it remote from their everyday lives. Nothing could be further from the truth.

Commodities are the things most of us use every day and depend upon.

They include:

1. Food,
2. Fuels of all kinds
3. Metals of all kinds, gold, silver, aluminum, precious metals
And much much more.

The thing is that these markets had been stable for years until after 2003 when congress and the Federal Reserve gave the big banks the right to speculate in these markets driving the prices in these basic areas sky-high and volatile and crash prone.

Gasoline in the US went from 1.25 are barrel to 4-5 dollars a barrel today

Wheat prices went up by over 3,000 percent, and therefore the price of many different kinds of foods all do to wall street speculator gambling in these commodities exactly like they do in derivatives. They have the money to monopolize markets forcing you and I to pay more to ensure their profits
irrespective of any "market conditions" and outside the real economy.

Finally the Federal Reserve in a terse statement is responding not to us but to other big corporations who too have finally realized that they have to pay these wall street fixed prices. They complained in numbers enough that the Fed has stated it will look into the situation they themselves created.

But wait is the Fed the monopoly organization of the big banks themselves.

So don't hold your breath. But note nothing happens in the US anymore unless the monied classes and organizations have a disagreement and decided to fight it out.

How does all this affect anything?
Arab Spring is and was directly started by increasing high fuel and food prices. The third world was hit by these banks rip-offs and Americans as well. The banks got to charge whatever they wanted to for these basics of life and the rest of us pay up or starve, borrow more money from them, or revolt while they offer austerity- here and in Europe. These are the facts of globalization that you will not see ever discussed in the press.

Meantime here are the details.

http://mobile.reuters.com/article/idUSBRE96J0AS201307 20?irpc=932

http://www.nytimes.com/interactive/2013/07/20/business/ marketsgraphic.html?_r=1&

http://mobile.bloomberg.com/news/2013-07-20/fed-reviews-rule-on-big-banks-commodity-trades-after-complaints.html

http://www.thesundaytimes.co.uk/sto/business/Finance/article1290197.ece?CMP=OTH-gnws-standard-2013_07_20

http://www.huffingtonpost.com/2013/07/19/wall-street-commodities_n_3625750.html

http://www.nytimes.com/2013/07/21/business/a-shuffle-of-aluminum-but-to-banks-pure-gold.html?pagewanted=all

http://www.washingtonpost.com/opinions/harold-meyerson-big-banks-dangerous-commodity-monopolies/2013/07/23/c310683e-f3c6-11e2-9434-60440856fadf_story.html?tid=pm_opinions_pop

7/23/13

Wall Street moves to head off financial transaction tax

http://www.opednews.com/articles/Edward-Snowden-and-Financi-by-Dean-Baker-130723-147.html

www.ingramcontent.com/pod-product-compliance
Lightning Source LLC
Chambersburg PA
CBHW051736170526
45167CB00002B/954